The Fastest Game on Two Feet

AND OTHER POEMS ABOUT HOW SPORTS BEGAN

by Alice Low

illustrated by

John O'Brien

Holiday House / New York

To Kathy . . . for everything
With love, A. L.

For Linda
J. O.

Text copyright © 2009 by Alice Low
Illustrations copyright © 2009 by John O'Brien
All Rights Reserved
HOLIDAY HOUSE is registered in the U.S. Patent and Trademark Office.
Printed and Bound in China
The text typeface is Breughel.
The illustrations were done in watercolor over ink on Strathmore Bristol paper.
www.holidayhouse.com
First Edition
1 3 5 7 9 10 8 6 4 2

Library of Congress Cataloging-in-Publication Data
Low, Alice.
The fastest game on two feet and other poems about how sports began / by Alice Low ; illustrated by John O'Brien.—1st ed.
p. cm.
ISBN-13: 978-0-8234-1905-0
1. Sports—Juvenile poetry. 2. Children's poetry, American. I. O'Brien, John, 1953- ill. II. Title.
PS3562.O8769P54 2009
811'.54—dc22
2007013441

CONTENTS

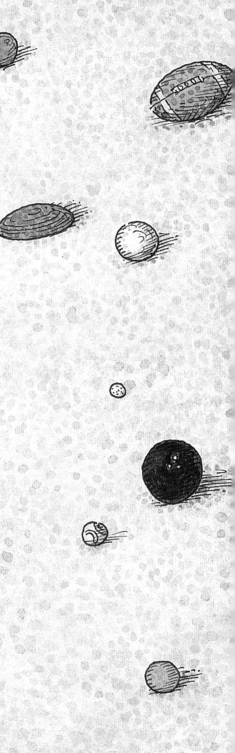

INTRODUCTION

Long, long ago, people all over the world played games with stones or ball-shaped objects.

Perhaps they hit the ball-shaped objects with sticks or with their hands, or kicked them or threw them, just as you might do if you were walking along. Many of the sports in this book are based on kicking, hitting, or throwing a ball. How many can you find?

Sports also sprang from people's need for survival—either to escape from animals and other dangers, or as religious rites to ensure the return of spring, or to bring sun and rain for the growth of the crops. The ancient Olympic Games were held in Olympia in Greece to honor Zeus, king of the gods.

As time went on, people developed sports, and they played them for fun. In fact, the word "sport" is short for "disportment," an amusement or a diversion.

These poems stress sports as fun, the creativity of some people who made them up, and how some sports changed through the years. Have fun reading all the poems and playing sports too!

If There Weren't Any Sports

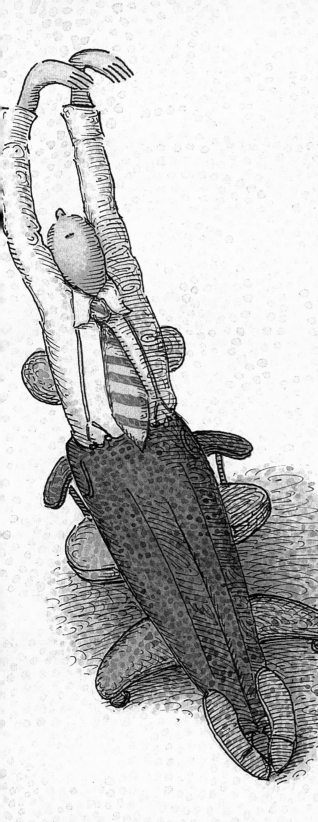

Supposing that there were no sports,
No tennis games on tennis courts,
No skates for skating on the ice,
No clubs to make a putt or slice.
No skis for skiing on the snow,
No boats to sail, no boats to row,
No football fields, no bats or bases,
No swimming meets, no running races.
No roller skates with wheels for rolling,
No bowling balls and pins for bowling,
No sticks for hockey or lacrosse,
No Frisbee disks to hurl or toss.
No soccer goals, no basketball,
Not any kind of ball at all!
No wickets, birdies, rackets—none!
What *would* you do to have some fun?

My guess is—if there were no sports,
You'd have a good incentive
To make them up, to use your wits,
You'd have to be inventive,
Like many people
In these pages
Who made up sports
Throughout the ages.

RUNNING

Running began as a form of survival and self-defense. Early humans were mainly vegetarians and seldom hunted animals; more often it was the other way around. No doubt people played running games early in human history in Asia, Africa, and other parts of the world. The Greeks glorified athletes, and the first Olympic Games featured running races.

They Ran for Their Lives

The early humans
Had to run.
They didn't do it
Just for fun.

They didn't do it
To compete
(With running shoes
Upon their feet).

They didn't do it
To stay thin,
To stay in shape,
Or just to win.

It wasn't just
A form of play,
For when they ran
They ran *away*.

If wild beasts
Were giving chase,
One *had* to win
That running race.

SKIING

The first skis were probably animal bones strapped to shoes and were used thousands of years ago in what is now Scandinavia and Asia to go cross-country in the snow. Next, wooden skis were used, and skiing as a sport began later in Norway with cross-country racing and ski jumping. In the 1940s ski tows popularized downhill skiing. The word "ski" means "snowshoe" in Norwegian.

A Way to Walk Through Snow

About five thousand years ago
When people tried to walk through snow
They sank in down to their knees,
'Til someone used her head (or his),
Some enterprising man or Ms.
Used animal bones for skis.

Those skis were strapped
To people's feet.
Today they would
Be obsolete
(Those skis, I mean,
Not his/her feet).

SWIMMING

The first people swam to keep from drowning and probably learned from watching animals swim. Guess how the dog paddle got its name. There was a natural progression from swimming as a means of survival to swimming contests for endurance and speed. The English were the first modern people to make swimming a competitive sport.

The Dog Paddle

When puppy dogs fall in the water
They know what to do to survive.
They paddle and churn,
And they don't have to learn
How to swim—so they come out alive.

But people who haven't learned swimming
Would sink like a stone in the sea
Or a pond or a lake
If they fell by mistake,
For we don't swim instinctually.

GYMNASTICS

Early forms of gymnastics were practiced in ancient Greece, Persia, India, and China. Acrobats—mostly women—performed in Egypt, and men and women vaulted over bulls in Crete. Gymnastics help develop strength, agility, balance, and coordination.

Fast on Their Feet

Gymnastics began
When a woman or man
Had to dodge all the dangers of long, long ago.
They would vault through the trees
And hang on by their knees,
Out of reach of the creatures below
In the forest,
Out of reach of those creatures below.

The years went on by
(And this *is* a far cry
From dodging those beasts who would eat them at will).
Young fit athletes in Crete
Who were fast on their feet
Became bull jumpers vaulting with skill—
And great daring—
Risked their lives despite vaulting with skill.

Now, gymnasts today
Sometimes study ballet,
Enhancing their grace and artistic routine,
Or they jump or they vault,
Or they may somersault
From a springboard, a big trampoline—
That takes daring—
But *no beasts* wait to wreck their routine.

BOWLING

Thousands of years ago people rolled stones at a target to knock it down. Games similar to bowling were played in ancient Egypt and Polynesia. But our modern game of tenpin bowling grew out of a religious ceremony that started in Germany around 300 CE.

From Aisle to Alley

Some Germans had a ritual
To make them free from sin.
'Twas very much like bowling,
For they set a stone a-rolling
Down the church aisle, and the object was
To hit a single pin.
Each churchman had a pin—his own,
He'd try to hit it with a stone.
By knocking down that single pin
A churchman would be free from sin.

Eventually that ritual
Became a sport for fun.
They didn't call it bowling,
Though they set a ball a-rolling
At a *group* of pins, sometimes they'd number
Up to thirty-one.
But usually those men would play
With nine pins—we use ten today—
So *ninepins* soon became the name
(And it became a betting game).

Then how did ninepins grow into
The game we play today
With ten pins? (That's *our* bowling,
Where we set the ball a-rolling.)
Well, the Dutch settlers brought it over here,
That's what some people say.
Ninepins, again a gambling game,
Was outlawed, so folks changed its name.
They added one more pin, and then
The game was legal once again.

And that is why, the legends say,
We bowl with ten pins to this day.

SOCCER

Soccer, called football in most countries, is the most popular game in the world. It was probably based on ancient kicking games, but one story used to be that the modern sport began in England from a game called kicking the Dane's head. The Danes had occupied England in the eleventh century, and when some British workmen found a Danish skull on an old battlefield, they enjoyed kicking it with all their might.

Kicking the Dane's Head

In the eleventh century
In England, it is said,
Some workmen found a Danish skull
And kicked that Danish head.
A group of boys (some barefoot)
Watched them kick the skull around.
It looked like fun, they tried it too,
But all too soon they found
That toes not covered by a shoe
Could end up very black-and-blue.
Because so many toes were bruised,
The bladder of a cow was used.

A hundred years or so went by,
The game spread far and wide,
And teams of rival villages
Met in the countryside.
The game had changed, it went like this:
The bladder was thrown down,
The goal—to kick it to the square
Inside a rival's town.
A mob scene of enormous size,
Accompanied by yells and cries!
And owners closed their shops and stores,
While shoppers fled, or stayed indoors.

This kicking game was dangerous
And often caused a riot,
And people begged authorities
For rules for peace and quiet.
They had to set some limits,
And they had to find a place
Where villagers could play the game
Within a marked-off space.
So fields were picked where games were played
With goal lines where the goals were made.
And through the years that sport became
A tamer worldwide kicking game.

LACROSSE

French settlers in Canada saw a game played by the Iroquois, Algonquins, Hurons, and other tribes. Often there were a hundred or even a thousand players on each side. The top of the stick used to catch the ball looked like a crosier (a staff carried by a bishop during religious ceremonies). The French words for "the crosier" are *la crosse*—which may explain where the French Canadians got the name. Canadians adopted the game, with changes, as their national sport in 1867. Men's lacrosse is now played with ten on a team, and women play with twelve.

The Fastest Game on Two Feet

Algonquin people used to play
A game they called baggataway.
Two teams, a hundred each, well matched—
Used sticks with netted loops attached
To toss and catch, up in the air,
A ball of deerskin stuffed with hair.
Because the goals were miles away
The game went on at least a day
And often two and sometimes three.
The ball must hit a rock or tree—
Or sometimes a far distant pole
Would be those young Algonquins' goal.
Baggataway was really rough
And helped to make contestants tough,
Which was the real point of it—
To train those players to be fit.

GOLF

There are many theories about the origins of golf. Scotsmen were playing a game called golf about 1500 or earlier, but a royal ban put a damper on the game. Later, King James IV played golf; and it was popular during the reign of Mary, Queen of Scots, who was the first woman golfer.

A Queen on the Green

Oh, Scotland's the land
Of the moors and the heather,
A country where golf came to be.
Those Scotsmen went golfing
In all kinds of weather,
They swung at a golf ball
Of feathers and leather.
The golf club was made from a branch of a tree,
Was whittled from wood of a tree.

But King James the Second,
He strongly objected,
And King James decreed a decree.
No golf was allowed
For the people neglected
To practice their archery,
Which, when perfected,
Would scare off an enemy coming by sea,
A fleet of ships coming by sea.

Along came a ruler
Named Mary, a queen
Of Scotland, a golfer was she.
She was the first woman
Who ever was seen
To swing with a golf club
Or putt on the green,
And golf became Golf with a capital G
In the reign of that queen
Who was keen on the green
About one thousand five fifty-three.

FIGURE SKATING

The first ice skates were small bones of animals used by people to get places. The word "skate" probably comes from *schaats*, a Dutch word. The Dutch, Finns, Norwegians, and Swedes were the first to use skates with wooden blades. In 1864, after steel blades were used, Jackson Haines, an American, introduced a freer style of figure skating. In the 1920s figure skating was given a great boost by a remarkable Norwegian skater, Sonja Henie.

Sonja Henie, Girl in White

Her name was Sonja Henie.
She was seven years or so
When her parents gave her figure skates
In Norway long ago.

She fell down when she tried them,
And her older brother said,
"Please, Father, take her skates away.
I fear she'll break her head."

But Sonja kept on trying,
For she was a stubborn girl.
She learned to glide and spin and jump
And execute a twirl.

She started winning championships
When she was only eight.
When she was ten she won again.
Oh, how that girl could skate!

She practiced seven hours a day
And studied ballet, too,
And fused ballet with skating
In a style that was new.

There isn't room to list
The countless titles that she won.
The Worlds, ten times, Olympics, three.
And still she wasn't done.

She took her ice show round the world
And traveled near and far.
She even went to Hollywood
To be a movie star.

And kings and queens and presidents
Acclaimed the "Girl in White,"
And Norway's King Haakon decreed
That she become a knight!

BASEBALL

Although people all over the world have played bat-and-ball games since primitive times, Alexander Joy Cartwright, Jr., a surveyor who lived in New York City, is often called the father of modern baseball. After work he and his friends played town ball, a game with a bat based on an English game called rounders. But in 1845 Cartwright headed a rules committee and drew up a new plan. The first recorded baseball game was played in 1846 in New Jersey and became popular in the East. The game was played by soldiers in the Civil War and soon caught on throughout the country. People call baseball America's national pastime.

A Man with a Plan

Alexander Cartwright was up at bat
In blue flannel pants and a tan straw hat,
Playing at a game with a bunch of men,
A game they called town ball way back then.

"Town ball is fun," thought Alexander C.
"But not as much fun as it *ought* to be."
So he hurried home and drew a new plan,
And that is how a brand-new game began.

RIGHT FIELD

FOUL LINE

COACH'S BOX

FIRST BASE

90'

PITCHER'S MOUND

9'

60.5'

FOUL LINE

45'

45'

5'

HOME PLATE

CATCHER'S BOX

3'

ON DECK CIRCLE

ON DECK CIRCLE

FOUL LINE

FOUL LINE

His Plan:
"Nine men on a team
And not one more.
Instead of five bases
We'll have four.
We'll place those bases
In a diamond square,
Ninety feet apart,
Which I think is fair.
Three strikes and you're out,
Three outs to an inning."
And that's how our baseball
Got its beginning.

Alexander Cartwright,
Alexander C.
A man
With a plan
That made history!

BADMINTON

Games with shuttlecocks were played thousands of years ago. Children in medieval England played a game like badminton called battledore and shuttlecock. Badminton got its name from the Duke of Beaufort's country estate, Badminton, in England. English army officers had played a game called poona in India, and they introduced it to England at a party at Badminton in 1873. Perhaps the day went like this.

The Game at Badminton

The Duke of Beaufort
Was a jolly old sport,
He invited some friends for a game of croquet
At his home, called Badminton
(Pronounce it like "kitten"),
But rain kept them indoors for most of the day.

They sat in the gloom
Of the duke's drawing room
With the weather decidedly drizzly and gray.
Said the duke, "Let's have tea."
Said his friends, "No thanks, we
Would sooner play poona, we'll teach you to play."

Said the duke, "'Pon my word!
Don't believe I have heard
Of that game, but I'll gladly oblige if I'm able."
They gathered together
Some corks stuck with feathers
And also a net, which they set on a table.

They hit those corks, *WHING*,
Using rackets with strings,
And the duke was transported, cavorted with glee
On that day at Badminton
(A place in Great Britain).
And when it was over, they all had their tea.

TENNIS

Credit goes to Major Walter Clopton Wingfield for publishing the modern rules of tennis in 1873, in Wales. He adapted them from court tennis, called *jeu de paume* in France, which started there in the thirteenth century. *Jeu* means "game," and *paume* means "palm" (of the hand). The ball was hit with the hand at that time. It was a favorite sport of French kings; but when it became a gambling game, Charles V of France forbade it for the masses.

That Gambling Game

Said Charles the Fifth,
The king of France
(Not Italy or Greece),
"This gambling game,
This game of chance
Must definitely cease.
It really makes me
Quite upset
That people use
The game to bet.
Before the game begins,
They put their money 'neath the net.
Stop tennis, I say!
Right now! Today!"

But people played it
Just the same,
Though tennis was a sin.
They absolutely
Loved the game,
They played it out and in.
They played in parks,
Cathedrals, too,
In cowsheds—
Just to name a few.
When monks had need of exercise,
You know what they would do?
Play tennis! They'd *play* . . .
And *play* . . . and *play*!

RUGBY

The game of rugby, it is said, came about accidentally in 1823. William Webb Ellis, a student at Rugby School in England, was playing football, which was then a kicking game like our game of soccer. Ellis failed to kick the ball and did something that was absolutely forbidden. Word got around quickly, and the following conversation might have taken place after that game at Rugby.

The Play at Rugby

"Oh, have you heard the news, my boys?"
"No, we have *not*. Please tell us!"
"A fellow on the football team
At Rugby named Bill Ellis
Did something shocking yesterday.
He made a most outlandish play,
Unsportsmanlike, I heard them say.
A boorish fellow, Ellis!"

"What did that fellow Ellis do?
Come, hurry up and tell us!"
"He made a most unheard-of run,
A thing that simply isn't done.
Perhaps he did it just for fun.
Unmannerly Bill Ellis!"

THIS STONE
COMMEMORATES THE EXPLOIT OF
WILLIAM WEBB ELLIS,
WHO WITH A FINE DISREGARD FOR THE RULES OF FOOTBALL
AS PLAYED IN HIS TIME
FIRST TOOK THE BALL IN HIS ARMS AND RAN WITH IT
THUS ORIGINATING THE DISTINCTIVE FEATURE OF
THE RUGBY GAME

A.D. 1823

"What kind of fun did Ellis make?
Now right this minute, tell us!"
"You won't believe it, but that lad
Picked up the ball and ran like mad.
Oh, what a nerve that fellow had!
That silly Billy Ellis!"

"What happened after that, pray tell?
Was Ellis punished? Tell us!"
"He wasn't punished, not one whit.
His captain had an awful fit,
And criticized him quite a bit,
He'll never hear the end of it.
Poor fellow, Billy Ellis!"

Note: That criticism died down, however. That play at Rugby brought about a new and popular game. Decades later, Ellis was almost forgotten until finally Rugby School erected a monument giving William Ellis credit for the game of rugby.

FOOTBALL

In 1873 Harvard, Princeton, Columbia, Rutgers, and Yale planned to meet to decide on rules for intercollegiate football. (Their game of football meant kicking the ball with the foot, which we call soccer today.) Harvard withdrew because they played by different rules than the others. Instead, Harvard played McGill University, which played rugby football, an English kicking game that also allowed tackling and running with the ball, which was oval.

A Decisive Match

Oh, Harvard was a stubborn team,
They said they wouldn't play
The other college football teams
Unless they played *their* way.
For Harvard played by different rules
Than any of the other schools.
(As stubborn as a bunch of mules
Was Harvard's team that day.)

Then Harvard asked McGill to play
(From Montreal they came),
But they played football *their* own way,
And rugby was its name.
Now what was Harvard going to do?
McGill, you see, was stubborn too
And hoped to play by rules *they* knew.
(I'm sure you'd do the same.)

Well, both teams gave a little bit,
And each team had its will.
They played one game by Harvard's rules,
The other by McGill's.
And Harvard found McGill's game fun,
They'd pick the football up and run.
(I won't go into which team won
Or which had better skills.)

What matters in the end is—
That the football played today
Is based upon that rugby game
That Harvard learned to play.

BICYCLING

It took a long time for the bicycle to evolve into a machine that could be used for fun and racing. One story went that Count de Sivrac invented the first crude bicycle in France. It had wooden wheels and no pedals! They came later. Not until rubber tires were used in 1868 and, more important, pneumatic tires in 1888, did biking become a popular sport. *Bi* means "two," and *cycle* means "circle."

No Pedals, No Medals

The thing about bikes
That most everyone likes
Is that pedaling's faster than hiking.
You can cover more ground
With the wheels going round,
Which is why there's a liking for biking.

Now this biking began
When a clever young man
Made a new thing for self-propelled motion
With a wheel front and back.
He was named de Sivrac
And resided in France 'cross the ocean.

But there's hardly a mention
About his invention,
That man didn't get any medals.
Though his bike had two wheels
It was hardly ideal,
For de Sivrac forgot one thing—pedals!

If you wanted a ride
You would push with your feet,
And you'd sit on a crossbar
Instead of a seat.
You would roll on a bit,
But you couldn't go fast,
So de Sivrac's invention
Was not bound to last.
But he did invent something
That was self-propelled,
Though it certainly didn't
Propel very well.
Though his bike had no pedals
We owe him a lot,
Despite the importance
Of what he forgot.

BASKETBALL

In the winter of 1891 James Naismith was an instructor in physical education. His students were bored indoors, marching around and doing calisthenics. His boss told him to think of something better. Indoor versions of soccer and lacrosse were too rough, so he tried to think up some other kind of ball game. At first, all he knew was what he didn't want.

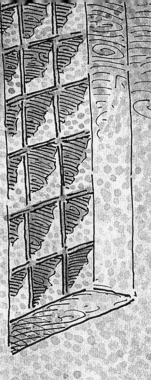

James Naismith's Predicament

I don't want a game
Where you run with the ball,
For someone would tackle
And someone would fall.

I don't want a game
With a ball that you kick,
Nor a game with a ball
That you hit with a stick,

Nor a game that's so rough
That you tumble and roll.
But I *do* want a game
Where you aim for a goal

With a ball big enough
You can pass it with ease
And a goal that hangs high
As the gym balconies

And making the goal
Takes great accuracy.
Now, what can I use
For the goal? Let me see—

I *could* hang some boxes
Up high with some ties,
But none of these boxes
Is quite the right size,

For some are too small
For the ball to go in
And the big ones would make it
Too easy to win.

I've got it! Peach baskets!
Just right for my game.
And now all I need
For my game is a name.

Now, what shall I call it?
I don't have a clue.
PEACHBALL? Or PEACHBASKET?
No, neither will do.

But "ball" is important,
And "basket" is too.
Why, BASKETBALL! Yes . . .
For my game that's brand-new.
"BASKETBALL! BASKETBALL! Wooo!"

SURFING

Surfing is an ancient sport. It was popular in Hawaii among chiefs and kings, as well as commoners, including women and children. But the man who helped popularize surfing in the modern world was Duke Kahanamoku, an outstanding Hawaiian swimmer and surfer. One day in the early 1900s, it is said, he made a legendary ride.

Duke Kahanamoku's Ride

On that day at Waikiki
  In Hawaii by the sea
    There were giant waves that seemed to reach the sky.
    And of all the surfers there
    There was one who took the dare.
    Duke Kahanamoku knew he had to try.

First he paddled on his board,
While the waves around him roared,
'Til he saw a wave that cried out to be tried.
It had speed and it had power,
And the wave was like a tower;
But he knew that wave was meant for him to ride.
When he stood up he was gliding,
He was soaring, he was sliding
Like tobogganing at top speed down a hill.
And he rode that wave to shore
For a mile and maybe more.
Oh, the day he caught "The Big One" was a thrill.

SKATEBOARDING

Skateboarding took a while to catch on after the first crude boards of the 1950s. The wheels broke apart or skidded, causing many accidents; and the boards were not maneuverable enough to control. Then in the early 1970s Frank Nasworthy used polyurethane wheels, which gripped the ground, were stronger, and gave new life to skateboarding. Here's how some people say it all started.

The Fastest Water Ski on Earth

What on Earth could the surfers do
When there was no surf to ride on,
When the sea was still
And they missed the thrill
Of an ocean wave to glide on?
One surfer fitted a water ski
With some roller skates for motion,
And he rode downhill
Using surfing skill
That he'd learned from the rolling ocean.

Though the fastest water ski on Earth
Was a clumsy, crude creation,
Still it hit the mark
For it lit the spark
Of a craze that swept the nation.

FRISBEE

College students played a game of tossing around pie tins; then in 1948 Walter Frederick Morrison designed a plastic disk modeled after a pie tin and sold many in California. He called it Morrison's Flyin' Saucer. The Wham-O Manufacturing Company bought the design and launched the Pluto Platter in 1957. Wham-O's owners later adopted the name Frisbee after they heard East Coast students use that name for their pie tin game. The owners did not know the origin of the name and spelled it wrong. Frisbie was the name of a company that made pies and pie tins.

A Pie Plate in the Sky

Sing a song of Frisbie,
A pie plate in the sky.
Hungry college students
Purchased a pie.
When the pie was eaten
One hurled the plate away.
Another caught it, wasn't that
A super game to play?

Sing a song of Frisbie,
An old pie company.
Their pie tins started off a game
That's fun for you and me.

Note: Could be sung to the tune of
"Sing a Song of Sixpence"

Author's Note

I like museums, especially the Metropolitan Museum of Art in New York City, where I'd gone sketching with my elementary school. One day decades later, I stopped to look at a marble sarcophagus from Roman times. There was an interesting figure sitting on an animal—I went closer to read the label. *The Badminton Sarcophagus*, it said. Badminton! I thought. Did that have anything to do with the sport I used to play? It must. Such an unusual name! I'm going to look it up. And I did—and it did. Though it was Roman, carved in Italy, it had been owned by Badminton House in England.*

After I did research on the game and how it started, I wrote a poem. And then I wanted to know how other sports had started, and still others; and here they are, poems about many sports.

Did I like sports? Yes—very much! I went to camp for years, and learned to swim and to play tennis, softball—and badminton. Art and writing were other interests and were encouraged at school—we wrote, illustrated, and even bound short books, and wrote poems and songs, which I loved—and still do.

And at home some of my mother's friends were artists, writers, editors, and publishers. I valued books. One that stands out is *A Book of Americans*—a collection of poems about explorers, presidents, and history. I didn't know I was learning; I was just having fun reading. Eventually all these things combined; and here, many years later, is the result.

While doing research for this book, I noted that not all researchers who wrote down what happened agreed. And occasionally they were wrong! For example:

Abner Doubleday invented baseball in Cooperstown, New York. No, no, no, that is not so (but people used to give him credit for it, and that is why the Baseball Hall of Fame is located there!). Abner Doubleday, a Union Army general, may have accomplished other things, but none of them had to do with baseball. Baseball was based on several old games, and Alexander Cartwright, Jr., played a key role in setting down some important rules of the modern game—for example, the distance between bases and having three outs per inning. He was elected to the Baseball Hall of Fame as a pioneer of baseball in 1938, and in 1953 the U.S. Congress officially recognized him as the inventor of baseball. But even as I write this, I read a book saying that some think that Daniel "Doc" Adams helped draw up those first rules! But Alexander Cartwright gets the credit in the Baseball Hall of Fame.

* The museum now labels the sarcophagus as *Marble Sarcophagus* (with accompanying information about Badminton House). It can be found in the Roman Gallery.

Other Anecdotes

Only males competed in the ancient Olympics. Unmarried girls were allowed to watch the races of the men and boys, whereas married women caught watching the men and boys race could be put to death. Unmarried girls also had their own competition—foot races in honor of the goddess Hera, wife of Zeus. This festival occurred every four years, also at Olympia, but at a different time.

Have you ever known anyone who has run a marathon? And have you ever wondered where that word came from? Marathon is a place in Greece where a famous battle was fought—the Greeks defeated the Persians. A messenger named Pheidippides carried the news of victory to the Greeks in Athens, running about 26 miles at great speed, and that is the distance of a footrace called a marathon. No, no, no, that is not so! He actually ran a much greater distance, and for a different reason. Nevertheless, that confused legend is the basis for the distance of the marathon in the first modern Olympics, in 1896. And the exact distance marathoners run today—26 miles, 385 yards—became standard after the British, hosts of the 1908 Olympics, decided to have the race start and end where the British royal family could see the runners conveniently.

Many years after those days of human dog-paddling, swimming became a competitive sport. In 1844 the Swimming Society in England invited an American Indian group to London for a swimming exhibition. The styles were very different. The English swam the breaststroke rather slowly; but the Indians "thrashed the water violently with their arms, like the sails of a windmill and beat downward with their feet," according to one onlooker. Years later the Indians' rapid stroke re-emerged in Europe as the crawl!

The word "trampoline" is based on the Spanish word for "diving board," *trampolin*. George Nissen, a gymnast from the United States, invented a device for bouncing up high. When he showed it off in Mexico, he liked the sound of the word and added *e*.

In 1925, Duke Kahanamoku, the famed Hawaiian surfer, rescued eight people from heavy surf in Newport Beach, California. They were fishermen whose boat had capsized. He used his surfboard to make many fast trips from shore to boat to shore. This was the beginning of lifeguards using surfboards to help save people from drowning.

TIME LINE

c. 5200 BCE – Nine stone pins, which are believed to have been from a bowling game, are placed in the tomb of an Egyptian child.

c. 2500 BCE – Egyptians practice swimming, for fun.

c. 2000 BCE – This is the age of the oldest skis, found in bogs in present-day Sweden and Finland. Also, the oldest form of ice skates that have been found are believed to date from this time period.

776 BCE – Time of the first written records of the ancient Olympics in Greece.

206 BCE – The Chinese play a game like soccer, called tsu-chu.

14th century – Canadian Indians play precursor of lacrosse, with masses of people on each side and goals miles apart.

1777 – English explorer James Cook writes of seeing surfing in Tahiti.

1846 – The New York Nine beat the Knickerbockers, 23–1, in the first officially recorded baseball game using Alexander Cartwright's rules.

1860 – Sondre Norheim (sometimes spelled Nordheim) of Norway uses roots and tree branches to make a ski binding that goes around the heel, making ski jumping possible and winning the first known ski-jumping contest.

1877 – The first Wimbledon tennis championship is held, although not until 1933 does a player dare to wear shorts.

1896 – Women begin to shed some of the restrictive clothing of the day, such as long skirts and corsets, so they can ride bicycles. Susan B. Anthony says that "the bicycle has done more for the emancipation of women than anything else in the world."

1899 – George Grant, a golfer who was one of the first African Americans to graduate from the Harvard dental school, receives a patent for a better golf tee. Strangely, two other dentists have also received patents for golf tee designs!

1905 – President Theodore Roosevelt convinces Harvard, Yale, and Princeton football representatives of the need for safer rules. Otherwise, the brutal, sometimes deadly, game might not have been preserved.

1908 – Figure skating first included in the Olympics, in London (indoors, of course!).

1950s – "Pinboys" no longer needed to set up the bowling pins, as automatic pin-setting machines come into use.

1962 – Wilt Chamberlain scores a record 100 points in an NBA basketball game.

1963 – First skateboard contest is held at Pier Avenue Junior High School in Hermosa, California.

1967 – High school students in Maplewood, New Jersey, invent Ultimate Frisbee—a combination of Frisbee, football, and soccer.

1967 – First woman runs the Boston Marathon with an official number, although she registered using just her first and middle initials, so it wasn't known she was female. When the race director found out, he tried to have her removed from the course!

1975 – Bob Hall is recognized for completing the Boston Marathon in a wheelchair, and a wheelchair competition has been included in the marathon every year since.

1976 – Nadia Comaneci of Romania receives the first ever perfect 10.0 score in gymnastics in the Montreal Olympics, although the display couldn't show it because it wasn't equipped to show a score that high!

1995 – The first Extreme Games (now called the X Games) in Rhode Island and Vermont include skateboarding, biking, and in-line skating.

2000 – The trampoline is included as part of Olympic gymnastics competition for the first time.

2005 – A badminton player from China sets a record for a "smash" of the shuttlecock—206 miles per hour.